Sam Has 2 Homes

Dedicated to Femi

On a beautiful spring day, Sam's alarm clock rang at 7:00 am. As it did every weekday at Mom's.

Today was extra special however, because she was going to see her dad after school.

"I have to pack," she said to herself excitedly as she jumped out of bed.

"There are so many things I would like to show Dad, and I'll need to figure out what to take with me," she said as she started to pack her bag.

"Oh, there are my new football boots, I can practice in these with Dad."

"And there's my new RC car," she thought aloud as she scratched her head.

"I want to show Dad my new drawings!" she said as she rolled a stack of paper that barely fit into the bag. That was when Sam realized she had a problem.

Her bag was filling up quickly, but she still wanted to pack other things. Her favorite blanket. Her T-Rex plush. Her glitter pen collection. Her brand-new sports jersey that had her name on the back.

Feeling a little overwhelmed, Sam sighed and said, "I need to figure out which of these things to take and which to leave."

Just then Mom called out to her, "Food is ready, Sam! Come and eat!"

Sam hurriedly closed her bag and went downstairs to see that Mom had made her favorite breakfast — crepes! But Sam was so excited and anxious that she could hardly eat.

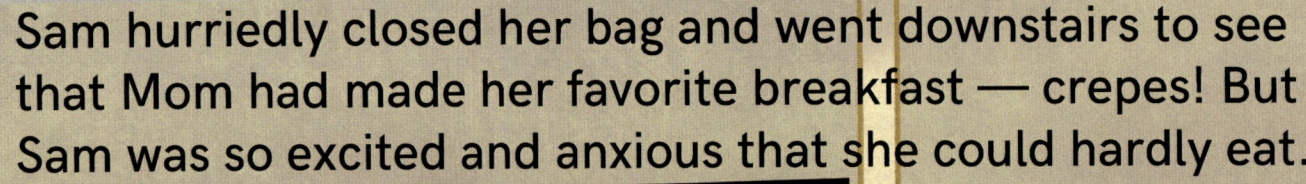

"Just one crepe please! I'm not that hungry," Sam said to Mom.

"Ok, give me a big hug before you leave," Mom said as she stretched her arms to Sam.

When Sam got to school, she opened her bag and realized immediately she had forgotten her T-Rex plush at Mom's.

"Oh no!" Sam said in disappointment.

"I don't like living in two homes. I want all my things in one place!" Sam said to herself angrily.

She had started off her day with a lot of excitement about seeing Dad. Now there were many other mixed feelings coming up that she didn't understand, but she knew she didn't like any of them.

During crafts class, Dennis and Sam were sharing a table when Dennis reached for Sam's scissors.

Sam immediately grabbed the scissors away from him and snapped, "NO! You can't have my scissors. Go get your own!"

Sam immediately felt sorry because she knew she had hurt Dennis' feelings. She just felt so angry and upset today, but she resolved she would not take her very strange day out on anyone else.

After school Sam was playing in the playground when she spotted Dad walking into her school. Sam was happy again! She ran as fast as she could to hug him.

As they were heading home, Sam remembered all the mixed feelings from the day and asked, "Daddy, why do I have to wait so long to see you every time?"

"Because your Mom and I don't live together anymore. You spend a week with Mom and afterwards a week with me," Dad replied.

"But you used to, so why can't you just come back?" Sam pressed further.

"Adult relationships can be complicated. Some people get together and start off wanting similar things. But as they grow, they realize this isn't the case anymore. And this makes them unhappy," Dad responded.

"Sometimes that means living separately and talking through it. It's a big change right now, I know. But in the end it'll make us all better and happier," Dad continued.

"You always tell me to talk it out when I'm upset with my best friend. Why can't you and Mom just figure it out in the same house? Was it something I said or did?" Sam asked.

"Oh no. Not at all. You have done absolutely nothing wrong. We both love you very much and want the best for you. At the moment while we figure it all out, you'll have to have two homes."

"Well, I don't like it because I can't do anything to help." Sam burst into tears as they walked through Dad's door.

"It's okay to feel sad and angry," Dad said. "What you should know though is we both love you very much and it's not your responsibility to fix our problems or make us feel better."

Sam felt a bit happier and started to show Dad the things she had brought in her backpack.

"You know what? Let's have jollof rice for dinner tonight," Dad suggested. Sam smiled. It was her favorite dinner meal.

The next day Sam's alarm rang at 6:30 am. A little earlier as Dad lived further out from her school than Mom. She woke up feeling much better than the previous day.

She was going to be at Dad's for a while and was excited to ride her bicycle here. But she also looked forward to the smell of freshly baked pastries from the cafe downstairs at Mom's.

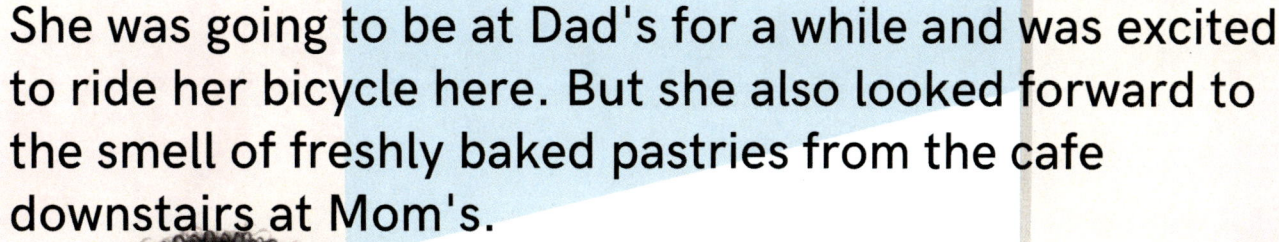

"There ARE benefits to having two homes after all," Sam thought to herself.

"Can I ride my bike before I head to school?" asked Sam after she got ready.

"Sure, I'll race you down the road and back," said Dad.

About the Author

Jide E. Fawole takes a contemplative approach to storytelling for children. His writing reflects his aspirations to take young minds on adventures where they can learn, discover and appreciate the beauty of everyday life. He hopes to inspire children to do big things through his Little Hero Adventures series.

Driven by a passion for life, adventure and exploration, Jide works as a public health professional and spends his free time playing basketball, football, cycling, swimming and motorbiking. He enjoys music and is a DJ.

Jide lives in Zurich, Switzerland. Sam Has Two Homes is his first children's storybook.

© 2023 Kunda Kids Ltd

Sam Has 2 Homes
Written by Jide E. Fawole
Illustrated by Francis Ude & Ramos Victor
Art direction by Chike Obasi

First published in 2023 by Kunda Kids Ltd

All rights reserved. No part of this book may be reproduced in any form by any electronic or mechanical means, including information storage and retrieval systems, without permission in writing from the author and publisher, except by a reviewer who may quote brief passages in a review.

A CIP catalogue record for this book is available from The British Library.

ISBN 978-1-7394149-1-7

Complete your Kunda Kids collection
Kunda Kids is a multi-award-winning EdTech and Media specialising in diverse and inclusive stories aimed at raising the next generation of global citizens.

Scan the QR Code to explore more at www.kundakids.com

Manufactured by Amazon.ca
Bolton, ON

36676744R00021